MW01137467

Living Purple Publishing
8469 S. Van Ness Avenue, #7
Inglewood, CA 90305

ISBN   978-0-9968311-5-4 (Paperback)

For more information about *Real Estate 100* please visit
www.realestate100.net

Published by Living Purple Publishing

REAL ESTATE 100
The Teen and Millennial Investment Blueprint

Anthony Lee & Lisa Puerto

I would like to first dedicate this book to my Beloved Grandmother Florence Robinson Morton who passed away July 21, 2015.We Love you and miss you *Mom-Mom*.

Secondly, I like to dedicate this book and my entire existence to my Mother my rider, my #1 fan who has always shown me unconditional love. To my Father, my best friend, the one who taught me how to be a man and showed how to be a true hustler; letting me work with you washing cars in the 1st grade and helping me start my landscaping business at the age of 12.

To my Son: I hope when you look back and see this you can say I made you proud. You have taught me true patience and what life goals are truly for. Stevi Adams soon to be Stevi Lee (at the time of this book release) thank you for always supporting my dreams and loving me as I am!

Lastly, I want to thank you, the reader, for purchasing this book. On behalf of the Real Estate 100 organization we hope that this book helps you get started on your real estate investment journey. *Remember It's Not That Complicated*, its just the beginning for you and your Real Estate Goals.

-Anthony Lee

To You, the reader, creator, and innovator of your destiny.
Your legacy awaits you.
-    Lisa P!

CONTENTS

KEY TERMS

- After Repair Value
- Mortgage
- Flip
- Buy and Hold
- Points
- Fico Score
- Rent
- Renting
- Lease
- LLC
- Equity
- Investment
- Investor
- Cash Flow
- Appreciation

WHERE DO WE BEGIN REBUILDING?

Hey there,

Welcome back or if you're new to the Real Estate 100 movement; welcome to the fam'
The Investment Blueprint brings us to a new era for this generation. It's time to do different. Think different. Be different. Better yet, just be great.

There are tons of great reading material out there on real estate investing, however, what is not available are the basics, *elementary* basics. If you have never been exposed to real estate investing, for example, come from a family of home owners, or are around real estate conversations daily other than what you see/hear on TV/radio, you may not have a clear understanding of how to get from renting to owning.

So in this approach, we are leveling up from the first book *Real Estate 100: The Teen Home Buying Experience* which covers basic real estate terms and concepts…and a recommended read if you haven't read it yet, IJS ☺

We now are introducing you to the possibility of not just ownership but building a legacy from it. Are you working for your last name? How personal is this to you? Because it needs to be!

It's thinking about home ownership in another way, which may or may not be for you. Sharing that information here is what drives us, so that you can then make an informed intelligent decision going forward. We could go on about the importance of real estate literacy, but you pretty much got the point. You are here for the 'how-to' and then apply it.

Let us continue with our shift in thinking …

Chapter 1
Get down with O.P.M
Financing with other people's money

Chapter 1
Get down with O.P.M.
Financing with o̲ther p̲eople's m̲oney

I was able to purchase my first property with $4,500, with the First Time Home Buyer program Some people spend this kind of money on cars, clothing or clubbing. So who's ready to build that Real Estate Portfolio?

Typically, financial professionals advise buyers to put down at least 20% of a home's purchase price. But as a first-time home buyer you can put down as little as 3.5%. Obviously, this should help get you started even sooner.

If you do need a mortgage, you might consider living in your investment property to take advantage of owner-occupant interest rates. You don't have to live there forever, either (that's niceeee). Lenders typically require just one-to-two years of residency to lock in the lower rate for the remainder of the mortgage. Owner-occupied interest rates are much more favorable than secondary home or rental property loans.

For those fortunate enough to purchase multiple income properties simultaneously, it's important to choose the right financing. However, how much do you need for your first deal?

Not everyone's situation is the same. If you are like the majority of people, your parents are not just sitting on thousands of dollars. I had to start my business from what I like to call from the muscle.

Think about the times you will have the opportunity to receive lump sums of money through your college refund, tax returns or some type of settlement. The major key is managing or putting that money to use to create more money instead of more debt.

Today 8:32 AM

Hey! I've been thinkin' about stepping up my real estate game...lol

Oh yea...you mean saving your turn-up $$$ and holding off on those 21" rims for your ride...LOL

I heard you mention that I can use the first-time buyer program to buy up to 4 units...is that real?

As real as it gets... call me so we can discuss your options

 Text Message　　　　　Send

Now you say, 'How do I get started? Where do I get the money from?' I would say the biggest key to getting started is to leveraging a full time job. This job will fund all or most of your first deal. These funds should cover your potential earnest deposit and any miscellaneous out of pocket expenses.

If you are like me and using the job to fund the first deal you will also need a somewhat decent credit score. A good starting point would be 600 and up, taking into consideration you may have not started building your credit history. Obtaining your first income property this way will allow minimum out of pocket expense. Which is called house hacking!

If the FHA loan is not an option, your next option would be to network and build relationships with local partners or hard money lenders. Hard Money Lenders[1] are not as bad as they seem.

---

[1] Hard Money Lenders are private or small groups that lend money based on the property you are buying and usually cost more than an average mortgage

They generally provide you with the full purchase price and renovation funds with the possibility of minimum out of pocket expenses. Through being in the Real Estate business I have been able to network and find private lenders through building relationships with other investors. The biggest warning I can give someone just starting out, is to make sure you understand all the fees and know your market so that you have enough wiggle room to always be able to pay your lender back on time.

Chapter 2
Picking your dime piece
How to choose your investment property

Chapter 2
Picking your dime piece
How to choose your investment property

Don't pick an investment property on projected assumptions, don't do it maannn...
I realized, as a first-time home buyer I could purchase an income producing property with the same money needed to rent a home or put a down payment on a new car. Before I went and purchased the so called dream car, I purchased a duplex (two-unit building) in West Philadelphia. If you are like me and have limited cash but have good credit there are loan options to help you become a homeowner/investor. *Sidebar: As an FHA buyer/owner-occupant, this property will be your primary residence.* So make it somewhere you will want to live.

Before purchasing consider the following:

- Will this property you plan to buy satisfy your lifestyle?
- Is the commute too long?
- Is the neighborhood not safe?
- Will you dread your time there because there's nothing to do?

These are all fair questions to ask yourself.

Pick a target area that you feel most comfortable with. Create a financial goal to help you achieve your financial freedom. My goal is to profit $200 per month after all expenses on each property. The rent is determined by location as well as the money being spent, for example, every 10k ($10,000) you spend your rent should bring you $200. Again as an example, for a 40k ($40,000) property you should have $800 in rent. Every area is different so your numbers and profits may need to be adjusted but at minimum you should always **cash flow** after your expenses.

Let me ask you a question: how long does it take you to pick out your clothes in the morning? I bet it takes longer than most people will spend doing the math on their next real estate investments. I just don't get it; people think the best deals are done on "intuition" and just buy something because it feels right.

Ugh. Please people!

If you don't have the right math going into a deal, you'll never get the right profit coming out of it. That deal you thought was incredible will turn out to be a thorn in your side for years to come and you'll join the ranks of the millions who have "tried" real estate only to give up too soon.

This is why I harp so often on getting a firm understanding of the math when buying an investment property. I don't care if you are buying your first or 100th property – you need to understand and do the math. That is my ultimate goal with this book: to help you learn to analyze a real estate deal so you can make the best investment possible.

●●●○○ 4G   **11:36 AM**   77 % ▭▶

‹ Messages   **Anthony**   Contact

Today 8:32 AM

Hey! So I came across this property I really like, I think it's a good deal...

How so? You ran your numbers or you choosing this dime piece based on how it looks alone??? LOL

Nah, I haven't ran my numbers, I was just looking at the low price

Check your numbers first, does it cashflow? Get at me so I can send you my spreadsheet

 Text Message   Send

> **Please, if there is one thing this year you read carefully and don't skim: let it be this.**

Below I'm going to walk you through the math I use to analyze a rental property, step-by-step. There are several primary factors I look at when analyzing a rental property, but the two most important are:

- Cashflow
- Appreciation

Cash flow is simply the money left after all the bills have been paid. Rent – Expenses = Profit

Appreciation is the equity[2] gained as the property value increases.

There are not a lot of great ways to estimate future appreciation without a crystal ball, so I generally choose to focus on the cash flow. After all, I am a buy-and-hold investor and I assume any appreciation is "icing on the cake" and not the only goal.

---

[2] Equity is the value in a property calculated by the difference of what the property is worth minus what is owed

So I'm going to focus this section on analyzing cash flow. Let's get started.

Cash flow is the money left over after all the bills have been paid. This is a simple enough definition, but it gets a lot of people in trouble. You see, technically, cash flow is:

Income – Expenses = Cash Flow

Okay, great. HOWEVER… where people tend to screw things up is the definitions. You see, income may include more than just the rent, and expenses will include more than just the mortgage. Let me give you a BAD example of calculating cash flow. You might say, "The mortgage is $800 per month and the property will rent for $1,000 per month – so my cash flow would be $200 per month."

False.

You see – you forgot about a lot of other expenses, including:

- Property Taxes
- Property Insurance
- Garbage
- Gas
- Electricity
- Home Owner Association (HOA) Fee
- Snow Removal
- Lawn Care
- Property Management

Now, some of these items are easy to calculate because you can simply call up someone important to find out about the cost. For example:

Taxes – Call your local county or look online at the county assessors page.

Insurance – Call your local insurance salesman and ask for a property insurance quote.

Water – Call your local water department

Garbage – Call your local trash provider

Gas – Call your local gas company

HOA Fees – Call the HOA president or hotline

Snow Removal – Ask local landlords what they pay or call a snow removal company.

Lawn Care – Ask local landlords what they pay or call a lawn care company for a quote.

Keep in mind, not all of these will apply to every property (or tenants may pay their own expenses) and some properties will contain more expenses than I've listed here. Don't get overwhelmed though – the more properties you look at in your local area the more you will understand what the "normal" expenses are ☺

Now, the numbers we just looked at are fairly easy to determine, but other numbers are more difficult to determine, like the vacancy, repairs, capital expenditures, and property management. But just because these numbers are difficult to nail down doesn't mean we shouldn't include them. Instead, we just need to use "averages." And for that, we look at those numbers as a percentage and translate those percentages into dollar amounts. Let's look at a few of the most common:

Vacancy: Properties are usually not rented 100% of the time; tenants move on and your property will likely sit vacant for extended periods of time. The length of time will depend on your local area and how good you are at filling those vacancies so I can't give you an absolute number. If you are unsure, try talking with some local property management companies to see what their typical vacancy rate is.

Once you know the vacancy rate, as a percentage, you can break down the percentage into a monetary amount. For example, if a property rents for $1,000 per month, and you believe the property will have a 5% vacancy rate, you simply take $1,000 x .05 to get $50. This is the amount you will want to include for your vacancy expense each month.

Repairs: Repairs are difficult to estimate because there are a lot of variables that come into play. A house that is 90 years old will likely have significantly more repair costs than a house built last year. A recently rehabbed house will also likely have fewer repairs needed than a home untouched for decades. Therefore, when looking at the cost of repairs, you will need to look at the property itself to determine how much you should allocate for repairs. Personally, I like to assume between 5% – 15%, depending on the condition and age of the property.

Keep in mind; this is a percentage averaged out over a long period of time, so it doesn't mean that every month you can expect 5%-15% of the rent to be spent in repairs. You may go 6 months without a single repair and then get hit with a $1,500 water leak. You just never know…smh.

Capital Expenditures: Also known as "CapEx" are those expensive "big ticket" items that need to be replaced every so often, but not every month or year. This could include roofs, appliances, driveways, plumbing systems, or any other large item you should be budgeting for. Many people ignore the CapEx in their analysis which I feel is a mistake. After all, if you were to earn $100 per month in cash flow for 10 years ($12,000) and then needed to put on a new roof for $12,000... what did you really accomplish in those 10 years? Like repairs, CapEx is difficult to estimate because it depends on the condition and age of your property. However, you can sit down and estimate how many years a roof will last, how many years an appliance will last, what the condition of your plumbing is, what a new driveway will cost, etc – and divide it out by the number of years. I generally like to assume the same number, between 5% – 15% for my CapEx.

Property Management: Property management (PM) companies typically charge a percentage of the rent, along with a fee to rent out a unit. These numbers can change based on your local area, but in my area, property managers charge 8%-10% of the rent and 50% of the 1st month rent when a unit is turned over. Rather than spending the time to get the EXACT cost of the property management based on vacancy rate, I will generally will just add 1% to whatever the monthly percentage is. In this case, the property manager charges 10%, so I'll call it "11%" assuming that extra 1% will cover the cost of their fee upon tenant turnover[3]. Now – what if you are going to manage yourself? S.T.I.L.L. BUDGET FOR MANAGEMENT. Heres' why: if you are successful (and you will be!) you cannot manage forever. There will come a day when you will have too many and you'll need to start using property management. What happens if you never budgeted for it? That's right: you lose all your cash flow. So whether you plan to manage yourself or not, budget for a property manager anyway.

Okay, at this point you should have a list of all the expenses and income sources for your property. Let's look at a hypothetical scenario: **123 Main Street is for sale for $100,000. It is a 3 bedroom home that would rent for $1,200**

---

[3] Tenant turnover refers to all costs associated witih moving a tenant out, updating unit and renting to a new tenant

per month. Breaking down the numbers, see Table 1.

[Table 1.] Property Address 123 Main Street Purchase Price $100,000	
Expenses	
Property Taxes	$120
Property Insurance	$55
Flood Insurance (if needed)	$0
Vacancy Rate - 5%	$50
Repairs - 5%	$50
Capital Expenditures - 5%	$50
Water - Tenant Pays	$0
Sewer - Tenant Pays	$0
Garbage - Tenant Pays	$0
Gas - Tenant Pays	$0
Electricity - Tenant Pays	$0
HOA Fees (if needed)	$0
Snow Removal - Tenant Pays	$0
Lawn Care - Tenant Pays	$0
Property Management - 11%	$110
Total Monthly Expenses	**$435**

We now know that our monthly expenses will average $435 per month. This number is known as our **Operating Expenditure**. Keep this in mind – it will come in handy in just a moment.

Now, we are not yet done in determining our cash flow. There is still one major expense we have not included: the mortgage. In the example above, we know the total cost of the property is $100,000, so our loan amount will depend on how much of a down payment we put. *Sidebar: If you are using a first-time buyer FHA loan you can put down 3.5% and it would be $3,500 for this example.* Let's assume we put 20% down. $100,000 x .20 = $20,000. Therefore, our loan amount would be $80,000 (because $100,000 minus $20,000 is $80,000) Now we simply plug in $80,000 into the mortgage calculator to determine our mortgage payment. The calculator will also ask for an interest rate and loan period. To determine the interest rate, ask a local mortgage lender what current rates are for the kind of property you are attempting to buy. Most residential loans (1-4 units) will allow you to go for 30 years, where most commercial loans (5+ units) will be 20-25 years. Plug those numbers into the calculator to determine your mortgage payment. In this case, we'll use an interest rate of 5.5% and a loan period of 30 years to discover our payment will be **$454.23**.

Finally, we have all the pieces of the puzzle to put together our cash flow analysis. We learned earlier that our total operating expense was **$435.00** per month, and now we know our mortgage will be **$454.23**. Let's add them together:

$435.00 + $454.23 = $889.23.

Now, we can determine our true cash flow by subtracting that number from the total income. In this case, our property will rent for **$1,200** per month. Therefore:

$1,200.00 – $889.23 = $310.77

On this example property, our estimated cash flow will be **$310.77** per month or **$3,729.24** per year. But… is this a g.o.o.d deal? Let's find out…**$310.77** per month in positive cash flow. This seems to be a good thing, but is it really?

The best way to determine if this is actually a good deal is by comparing it to something else. After all, this investment DID cost you money to buy it, right? You spent **$20,000** on the down payment, plus (let's say) another **$5,000** on the closing costs and yet another **$3,000** on the rehab to get the property 100% rent ready. So at this point, you have paid **$28,000**. So, is **$310.77** per month a good deal on a **$28,000** investment? This is when **Cash on Cash Return on Investment** comes in real handy. Cash on Cash ROI is a simple metric that tells us what kind of yield our money is making us based only on the cash flow (ignoring appreciation for now, because remember, that's just the icing on the cake ☺).

The Cash on Cash ROI is nice because it allows us to compare this investment to other investments, like the stock market or mutual funds. So let's do that. Cash on Cash Return on Investment is simply the ratio between how much cash flow we received over a 1 year period and how much money we invested. In other words: CoCRoI = Total Annual Cash Flow / Total Investment.

So using the example above:

CoCRoI = **$3,729.24 / $28,000 = 13.32%**

We have determined that this property should produce a cash on cash return on investment of 13.32%.

Is this good?

That's up for you to decide. Over the past few decades, the stock market has averaged around 8%, so I like to think 13.32% is a pretty darn good return. Additionally, this doesn't take into account the appreciation that will take place, the tax benefits you might receive, or the loan paydown that IS taking place (after all, every month the loan gets paid down a little more!) So JUST looking at cash flow, you are achieving a better than average return. However, as word of advice, only you can determine what a "good" return on investment is. The numbers are meant for comparisons.

Hopefully this write-up has given you the basic tools needed to start analyzing your own rental properties. After all, buying a bad deal is like getting into a bad marriage. Separation is difficult, expensive, and stressful. Don't buy a bad deal by not crunching the numbers, instead be sure to calculate ALL the numbers on your next investment property and shop smart!

Chapter 3
When to say deuces
Flip or hold your real estate investment

Chapter 3
When to say deuces
Flip or hold you real estate investment

Yo! You made it through. I know the numbers and math stuff was a bit much, but when you're dealing with money, it has to be broken down. I choose the buy-and-hold strategy because it is the most consistent stream of income for my risk tolerance. It's not the most exciting or lucrative game however done correctly it will be the retirement portfolio of your dreams. If you're going to be in buy-and-hold business decide whether you are going to purchase big properties, small properties, 2 bedrooms, 3s, or 4 etc. also referred to as your *mix*. I prefer 3 bedrooms because of the high demand from tenants and sellers looking to unload. This is where you will learn your risk tolerance in terms of what you are willing to handle. And it's fair to say that you may not know starting off, so there is only one way to find out – that is by doing. Then you can continue to draw the blueprint of what is best for you.

When it comes to beginners I strongly suggest using Section 8 or other subsidized housing. This will help decrease your chances of failure, and improve your profits by having guaranteed income from 1-2 year leases. Initially starting out due to their rent being guaranteed for 1-2 year leases. There are some good and bad tenants everywhere however the goal is to receive payment. The goal of becoming a landlord is to make money while you sleep and *ohh* what a better feeling than receiving money on the first of every month!

My goal is to buy single family properties and renovate them for under $50,000. For

Today 8:32 AM

...I had another question about that property I was thinkin' about buying....

What's up?

How long do I have to keep it before I can flip it?

That depends on your strategy. So you not buying to hold long-term, you wanna flip? Just call me so we can go over some options

 Text Message   Send

example House 1 is being sold for 60k. I would look at the property and deduct my renovation cost from 60k and use that as my starting point for the purchase price. Additionally, I make sure I am never into the property for more than 65% of the value once purchased and rehabbed. House 1: I purchase and rehab the property with total expenses all in at $50,000. Once my fees and closing costs are added my expenses become $55,000. Now, House 1 After Repair Value is $112,000, my goal is to never be all in for more than 65% which is $72,800. Keep in mind If I can keep my budget at $50,000 and my all in cost is around $55,000 I now have property with almost $15,000 in equity that can be used to build business lines of credit or cash out refinance. Please keep in mind this is a blueprint you can design or do this how you see fit.

There will be properties that you are going to flip for quick money. There will be those you keep for your portfolio. Find that balance as you become more comfortable with the approach. Continue to seek opportunities to build your wealth. There is nothing wrong with attaining wealth. Real estate done right provides a service to all in involved. There will be some hiccups along the way and this is where you are reminded that this may not be for you. But at least, you now know what it involves. It's easy to see how everyone else is ballin' on their real estate or income property, but be mindful that they are running it as a business! And in order to benefit from it, you have to t.h.i.n.k. and s.e.e. in that way. Hence, the term landlord.

Chapter 4
Is this for you – do you boo
Making a career out of real estate

Chapter 4
Is this for you – do you boo
Making a career out of real estate

We hear the words "Financial Freedom" thrown around, but what does it really mean? Is it just having or earning a lot of money? I know people who earn $800,000 a year and they are far from *free*! They are in businesses or jobs that own them. I also have met two different millionaires, one of whom owns multiple businesses and has more time/freedom than most. Do you want to be hands off from your business? Do you want to have true financial freedom ? Do you want to have unlimited TIME & freedom? Seeing that time is our most valuable commodity, why not make the most of it?

One of the keys to having freedom is to OWN the business and NOT let the business own you. *That is the mistake of so many of us small business owners.* We let the business own us. We don't mean to when we start out, but in a short time that is what happens if we don't make a conscious effort to avoid that trap. If we fall into it, we have no time for anything other than business and surviving!

It can be as simple as hiring a property management company to manage your real estate, or hiring contractors to do the work you might do yourself on your flips. This will provide freedom! Yes it costs money, but what can you do with the new time that you have found? Whatever you want! Ask yourself what is your time worth? For some the goal is to vacation, spend time with your family, build your business, buy more rentals, flip more houses, again, it's your time, do what you will with it.

Most new investors hear how great investing in real estate can be and they want to start buying property right away. For some the motivation is schedule freedom, financial freedom, or it could just be the fascination of what you see on Real Estate TV shows and seminars. For me the goal is to create enough monthly income so that I never have to work by need but by choice. However, as a former newbie (trust me I'm still just as new as you), I've just made a few more mistakes. I understand the frustrations of wanting to get started in real estate investing and not quite knowing what to do! As a new investor, reaching financial freedom can't happen fast enough. At some point I'm sure you will attend every local seminar, read every book and probably listen to every could-be real estate mogul you know.

You're not wrong for having these goals or feelings. You are right; there is a better way to live and a better way to run your investing business. It became apparent when I learned how some of the Big Dogs ran there companies. They didn't work the company!! They invested, by finding the right people to run the company. That's it! Is it really as simple as that? Not quite! To have companies run smoothly, you must develop systems and build relationships.

If you ask me, the biggest obstacle in starting anything new is to take the first step. Taking action, not just talking about it but actually being about it. You have to get out there and get yourself a little dirty. You can't win if you don't play and you only fail if you don't try. Please, don't be scared to fail your way to the top. It takes experience to be able to tell whether a business idea is good or not. It also takes some reasoning about what it means for a business idea to be good. Similarly, opening a restaurant may be a good business idea for some people, but not for most. So a business idea has to be highly personalized to the newbie to take advantage of their abilities, interests, passions, education, access to capital, connections, and much more.

Today 8:32 AM

You still out showing properties? I was thinking I might wanna come out there with you...

Almost done for the day. Let's set up a time. You can decide if you want to get into sales, flips, or something else in real estate...tons of options

I like the idea of being able to collect that rent check...need to stack n' build!

 Text Message   **Send**

Quite often, first time investors also make the mistake of trying to go too big with the idea right away. Some of the common business idea mistakes are to try to open a business that would require millions of dollars when they only have access to a few thousand dollars with which they can realistically start. It is good to have ambition, but some small wins are needed in order to build on them and go bigger.

If you hang around broke people, the *I'm going to do* versus *I'm doing*, or negative individuals what do you expect to learn or gain from them? Obviously, nothing. This Real Estate business is forever changing and forever growing. If I don't stress anything enough I would stress finding a coach or an experienced agent that has your best interest at heart. There is nothing wrong with paying for education, however if you have access to money; I would buy a house and learn from the mistakes. I've been able to locate a few experienced investors that help me analyze deals or provide insight. Which have all been created through relationship building. In every relationship there has to be give and take. *Fair Exchange* is what I like to call it. In every city there should be a mastermind or networking group where you can go for free or minimum cost. You can also search online networking events or meetups to find groups and events in your local real estate market.

Volunteering your time is also a good starting point. Volunteer your services/time whether it be big or small in order to learn from your experienced peers. I remember hanging flyers up for one investor just to have his time while dropping me off at the location to hand out marketing flyers. Another volunteer tactic may be to do office work for someone.

Sometimes real estate investing for beginners can seem a bit intimidating and it's easy to get lost in the lights and sounds of all the blogs, books, and television gurus with their slick hair, LOL. Before you start investing in real estate, remove the thought that you need to know everything before getting started.

However, you do need to understand basics. There are dozens of ways of becoming familiar and confident enough to get started. You can read books, which is my personal favorite thing to do or listen to audio books and podcasts that are free. There are even dozens of national and local real estate forums that can aide your learning process. Even if you didn't graduate on honor roll or struggled like me in staying focused, there are ways to learn this business when you commit to the lifestyle. Once I discovered Real Estate, it took over like a passion. I began reading for fun more and more. Then at one point, I was reading more books than I was watching TV... I felt like I read just about every book that I either was told about from another investor or suggested to read from another book. At last, I was able to understand the information being presented or discussed during the local Real Estate networking events.

Like anything else you have people who genuinely want to help you and you have others who are looking at you as prey. With Real Estate, you receive so many rewards that provides a sense of satisfaction through reaching your goals. Through networking you may find someone who would like to pay their accomplishments forward by *reaching one to teach one*. Such as assisting others through a jegna[4] (I got my first RE jegna through volunteering my time to assist him with cold calling in which in return he would help guide me through finding my next deal). You never know what you learn just by asking about someone's journey. They may just simply share their story of the good and the bad for you to take notes. Your local market place should have local networking groups or mastermind groups which can help you find that jegna. Just attend the meetings and be a fly in the room.

I'm not saying you have to get new friends but I am saying you can't learn how to be an auto mechanic or Poker play by associating with pet

---

[4] Jegna refers to an individual who is affirmed in their purpose and practice of life

groomers. If someone wants to help guide you it shouldn't cost you thousands of dollars, either. I made the mistake of paying so-called coaches and nothing came of it but listening to someone toot their own horn. If someone is going to guide you it should be genuine, each person should be bringing some value to the table. Don't think because you are new you don't add value. Again just starting out I only had time to offer so I "cold called" or delivered flyers for my jegna. In exchange he educated me on lead marketing and helped me navigate some of the steps towards getting my first and second deal.

Whatever it takes to get the knowledge!

Chapter 5
Real Estate
Establishing wealth and your legacy

Chapter 5
Real Estate
Establishing wealth and your legacy

Real Estate. Two words that make up something so powerful. We can easily take it for granted because we may not know its history. Or it might just be played out ... but the fact remains there is real value in it. Communities are built upon it, some have been destroyed because of it. We are all having a real estate experience. From the moment we open our eyes: to be grateful for the roof over our heads (residential real estate). The gas stations which we fuel our cars (commercial real estate). The grocery stores which we buy our goods and basic needs from (commercial real estate). The food and crops that are grown and processed for us to eat (agricultural real estate). The buildings and centers that process our products for consumption (industrial real estate).The schools or institutions we gather to learn (commercial real estate). The parks and amuzement parks we play in (commercial real estate). The clubs and lounges we hang out and vibe out to(commercial real estate). You get the point yet?

Your neighborhoods sit on land and are worth more than gold to those that can interpret calculating those numbers you learned in Chapter 2. So guess what? You have just been given a mad assist, and heads up! You get to decide which way this goes. Again, are you working for your family name? Investing does not have to be on a large scale. This is just one avenue to using the options available to you to your advantage. Start small, where you are. Draw up a plan, and you have us to call on. Build your team of solid

Today 8:32 AM

Anthony, I wanted to drop a quick thank you for the work you do.

No problem, the change starts with us. We know the information and we need to share it #eachoneteachone

...riight :)

We just keep building.

📷   Text Message   Send

partners that are like-minded. And then step forward.

We commend you for reading through. The next steps are up to you. You are not alone, we are here as advocates and a resource for you. This is how we build and win together. While we dived into pretty in depth topics of real estate investing on a basic level, there is more to it. Don't guess your way through it, reach out and learn more about things such as setting up LLC's and lease negotiations and much more. Together we can assist you in achieving your real estate goals.

Happy house hunting!

Anthony A. Lee

Lisa P.!

Super Investor & *Super Agent*ˢᴹ

Anthony A. Lee

Anthony A Lee has been a full time Pennsylvania

Real Estate
Professional
since 2013.
Lee's area of
expertise is
Residential

Properties. Providing the highest level of integrity and personalized service are the keys to Anthony Lee's success.

He has built his reputation on his ability to define the needs that are unique to each client. He utilizes the latest technologies, market research and business strategies, along with his drive, persistence, creativity and knowledge to exceed the expectations of his clients. Lee's real estate passion serves to invest his expertise and experience in his community, and he continues to expand his resources and network.

Anthony takes a distinguished approach to real estate, one that is built on personal touches, win-win deals and positive results. Many of his clients are Millennials and young professionals that need patience and guidance to create their blueprint of Real estate goals. He has formed partnerships such as, the Real Estate 100 movement Teen and Young Adult Home buying experience. These partnerships impact the clients and communities knowledge through expanding a nationwide collaborative in empowering communities with real estate resources of real estate, education and financial literacy.

To learn more visit **www.aleerealestate.com**
Connect and build on social media:
Facebook® @anthonyleerealestate
Instagram® @aleerealestate

Super Investor

Super Investor is modeled after our partner and member Anthony Lee who has been a positive image and has made great contribution in supporting students of all ages who are interested in learning real estate and entrepreneurship

Lisa Puerto, Super Agent℠

Lisa has been a California Real Estate Professional since 2006. Lisa epitomizes passion, integrity, energy, hard work, and creative service in every detail of her clients' real estate transaction. She has continued to increase her experience and knowledge  of real estate sales representing sellers, buyers, and investors in the residential market.

Lisa is widely known for her trailblazing book, **Real Estate 100: The Teen Home Buying Experience** (2015) which empowers the younger generations with real estate literacy.

Recently adding international speaker to her list of accomplishments. She is sought out from local and national entities as Advisory Council seeking to leverage real estate as part of their growth strategies. In addition to being featured in print and electronic media outlets, she has spoken on various real estate forums/panels, and community outreach events.

She is CEO & Founder of Real Estate 100 Youth Foundation Inc, a 501c3, as the nation's first real estate focused youth development nonprofit. **www.realestate100youth.org**

Trailblazing the way for the next generation, look out for her new online webshow *Ready, Set, Real Estate! With Lisa Puerto, Super Agent^{SM} - show* topics focuses on every aspect of real estate for the Millennials generation, the largest demorgraphic in American history.

To learn more visit **www.lasuperagent.com**
Connect and build on social media:
 Facebook® Twitter® Instagram® YouTube®
@lasuperagent

Super Agent ™

Super Agent[SM] is modeled after our CEO & Founder Lisa Puerto, who has spearheaded the #REALESTATE100 movement. She continues to traiblaze the real estate industry for young professionals and is a proponent of real estate literacy.

CPSIA information can be obtained
at www.ICGtesting.com
Printed in the USA
BVOW05s1706220817
492607BV00019B/87/P

9 780996 831154